by Shona Keith

A children's book
from
W H Allen
1979

Harry's granny loved knitting.

One frosty day she said to Harry, "Your fingers and ears look blue with cold - I will knit you a Balaclava helmet and mitts to match."

So she did, and Harry, who was very kind, said they were lovely.

Then Granny, who was always worried about Harry's health, said, "Harry, dear, you still look cold. I will have to knit you a warm jumper."

So she did, and soon Harry also had a new jumper – but it was far too big.

Harry was always very polite and told his granny it was perfect. Granny, who couldn't see very well, was delighted.

Of course, when Harry's friends saw him in his baggy jumper, hat and mittens they had a good laugh.

PARK

Then one day as Harry was walking home, he spotted a robin lying in the snow, frozen stiff and not looking at all well.

Harry carefully picked up the robin and tucked it up inside his baggy jumper to keep it warm.

By the time he reached home the robin had started to stir inside Harry's jumper.

A few hours later, the little bird was quite better, and Harry let it go from the kitchen window.

"Well," said Harry, "I don't care how silly I look in my baggy jumper - it certainly came in useful today!"

To this day Harry is proud to wear his jumper and wears it whenever he can.

He also wears his Balaclava helmet and mittens in case they come in handy too.

Now Granny is very busy knitting jumpers for all of Harry's friends.

Printed in Great Britain by
E Hannibal + Co Ltd, Thurmaston
Bound by Hunter + Foulis Ltd,
Edinburgh, for the publishers,
W H Allen + Co Ltd, 44 Hill Street,
London W1X 8LB

ISBN 0 491 02465 7 (cased)
ISBN 0 491 02319 7 (limp)

To Ian - for his encouragement